The Colonel has helper-programs for doing special jobs. One of these, the *Table Manager*, keeps track of the addresses where information is stored in the computer's main memory—its *RAM* (Random Access Memory). When the Bytes get to the CPU, the Table Manager reads their letters and looks up the address of the "FLOWER" program.

The Colonel leaves the CPU to fetch the "FLOWER" program from memory. On the way it runs into a *Bug*. A bug is a bad command—a mistake!—in one of the Colonel's helper-programs. The Bug sends the Colonel into a *loop*. A program is in a loop when it does the same commands (like "ADD 5 AND 5") over and over.

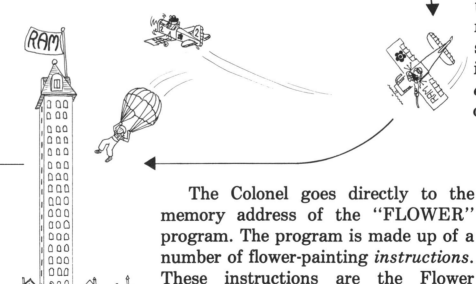

THE WORLD INSIDE THE COMPUTER

The Colonel looks at the computer *clock* to make sure everything is on schedule. The Colonel sees it is late and uses an *emergency interrupt* to get out of the loop.

Colonel fetches the Flower from memory and rushes them us to the CPU, then to the ube. A *bus* is a group of wires as a path for information to go e part of the computer to

The Colonel goes directly to the memory address of the "FLOWER" program. The program is made up of a number of flower-painting *instructions*. These instructions are the Flower Painters in our story.

Katie AND THE COMPUTER

by Fred D'Ignazio • Illustrations by Stan Gilliam

**For Janet Letts D'Ignazio
and Idelle Collins Gilliam**

Katie's father was waiting for her when she got out of school. He was very excited. "Katie," he said, "our computer came!"

"Oh, boy!" said Katie. "Can I play with it?"

"Sure," said her father, and they rushed home.

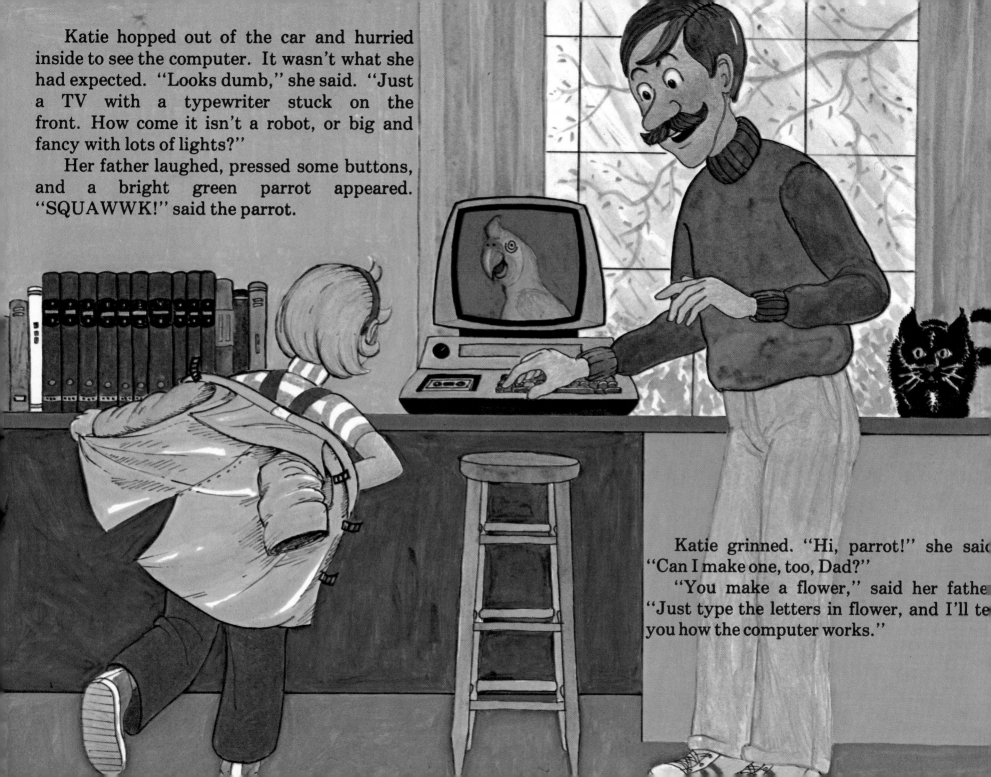

Katie hopped out of the car and hurried inside to see the computer. It wasn't what she had expected. "Looks dumb," she said. "Just a TV with a typewriter stuck on the front. How come it isn't a robot, or big and fancy with lots of lights?"

Her father laughed, pressed some buttons, and a bright green parrot appeared. "SQUAWWK!" said the parrot.

Katie grinned. "Hi, parrot!" she said. "Can I make one, too, Dad?"

"You make a flower," said her father. "Just type the letters in flower, and I'll tell you how the computer works."

FLOWE

"The world inside the computer is very, very small," Katie's father began. "There's a 'Colonel' in there who lives in a place called 'ROM.' When you send an order to the computer, the Colonel gets the order first. He runs off and tells the rest of the computer what you want done."

As Katie typed 'flower,' she leaned closer and closer to the picture screen. Then she lost her balance and fell forward. But instead of bumping her nose on the glass, she went right through it and began spinning and falling, just as if she'd tumbled off the top of a tall mountain.

Inside the computer it was snowing. As Katie fell, a snowflake as big as a house fluttered past her. Wow! she thought, I'm really getting tiny!

Suddenly the ground rushed up, and
Katie landed, "FLUMPFF!!," in a bank of
feathery snow. She blinked her eyes and saw
a curious-looking man in a fancy soldier's
uniform. "Hey! You're the Colonel!" she
cried.

"I *am* the Colonel," he boomed. "Wel-
come to the Land of ROM. It's part of
Cybernia, the world inside the computer. I'm
here to take your order."

Katie jumped up and said, "Let's make a
tower!"

"That's easy!" said the Colonel. "Come on, we'll round up some Flower Bytes and head to the CPU." He took off, charging through the deep snow. Katie chased after him.

The Colonel stopped suddenly, and Katie crashed into him from behind. "This is where the Bytes live," he said. "Each Byte has a letter or a number that's all his own." The Colonel reached for his bugle. "I use this to summon the *Flower* Bytes," he explained. "It only plays two notes, but I can arrange them into a special song for each Byte. Listen, and you'll see."

"BLEEETT!" burped the bugle. "BLAATT! BLEEETT! BLEEETT! BLEEETT! BLAATT! BLAATT! BLEEETT!" As the Colonel played, Bytes came running from the houses and leaped onto a bobsled. "Their letters spell a word," Katie cried in delight. "F - L - O - W - E - R. Flower!" She bounded off through the snow, and climbed into the front seat of the bobsled. "C'mon, Colonel!" she called.

The Colonel jumped onto the bobsled, and off it went, racing madly down the frozen hill. This is better than a roller-coaster! Katie thought, feeling happy, scared, and silly all at the same time.

The Colonel yanked a big gold watch out of his pocket and exclaimed, "We're overdue at the CPU! If these Bytes show up one second too late, Katie won't get her flower! Let's go now! Faster!! Faster!!"

The bobsled shot off the mountain, then slowed down and stopped with a "SHHHHUUUUUUUPPPPPP!" in front of a huge old train station.

"It's the CPU!" said Katie.

The Colonel sprang out of the bobsled and hollered, "All our orders go through the CPU! Come on!" He dashed inside, with Katie and the Flower Bytes close behind.

The inside of the CPU was big and busy. Excited chains of Bytes were everywhere, worming and wriggling around strange machines which clanked, swooshed and banged. "Those Bytes dancing over there are *Letter* Bytes," The Colonel said. "They're just like the Flower Bytes. They hold hands and make new words. See the *Number* Bytes riding on our Adding Machine? That's where we make new numbers."

"A ferris wheel!" Katie cried. "Can I ride on it!?" When no one answered, she turned around and saw the Colonel and the Flower Bytes rush into a crowd of skateboarding Number Bytes, then disappear. She chased after them.

In the center of the CPU was a mountain of paper behind a long oak table filled with filing boxes. A frail, frazzled-looking man with fists full of paper scraps dashed back and forth between the table and the paper mountain. To get the man's attention, the Colonel smacked him on the bottom with the flat part of his sword. In a bullhorn voice, he declared, "AH - TEN - SHUNN!! Table Manager!!"

The Table Manager popped up like a jack-in-the-box and saluted the Colonel. "My! My! My!" he cried, "the faster I go, the behinder I get!" Pointing to Katie, he said, "That girl's father is running me ragged. The mountain of paper behind me is full of addresses he wants filed on my Address Table. But no matter how quick I file 'em, that darned mountain keeps getting bigger. Why, I ..."

"This is top priority!" the Colonel growled. The Bytes stepped forward, one at a time. "F!" yelled the first Byte. "L!" cried the second. "O!" screamed the third. "W!" called the fourth. "E!" shrieked the fifth. "R!" shouted the sixth.

"Flower!" the Table Manager said. "You want the Flower Painters' address at RAM Tower! It hasn't been filed, but I know just where to find it." He rolled up his sleeves, climbed a step ladder, and dived like an eagle into the huge pile of paper. After some mumbling and crunching, the pile sprouted an arm and a hand clutching an address.

Katie ran over, climbed up the mountain and grabbed the address. The Colonel wheeled around in front of the Flower Bytes. "DIS — Missed!" he thundered. He raced to an airplane marked with a flower and climbed in. Glancing at his watch, he cried, "Where's the pilot?"

"Gone!" shouted the Table Manager. "Out on a call! She won't be back for another ten seconds."

"I can't wait!" the Colonel bellowed. "Katie, hop in! I'll fly. You navigate." As the Colonel and Katie flew away from the CPU, the Table Manager called to them: "Watch out for the Bug! I hear it's a monster!"

"A Bug!" Katie shouted. "What kind of Bug!?"

"A mean and tricky Bug," said the Colonel.

"Where'd he come from?" Katie asked.

The Colonel snorted. "When my helpers like Table Manager were created, one of them was to be a Traffic Cop who would help direct the airplanes from the CPU to RAM Tower. Something went wrong. The Traffic Cop never came. Instead we got a Bug—a huge and horrible creature that attacks our planes."

"Yuck!" Katie said with a shiver. "I hope we don't run into him."

They swooped around the corner of a tall building, and there was the Bug!
"Come here!!" he roared. "Let me help you!!"
"Don't believe him," whispered the Colonel. "He's trying to trick us!"

The Colonel dived the plane between the Bug's legs, but the Bug lassoed them with his sticky bubble gum rope, and began reeling them in like frightened flounder. The Colonel jammed the gas pedal to the floor, and in a loop they spun, like a merry-go-round gone crazy. The Bug pulled them closer and closer to his hungry jaws.

Katie was frozen with fear, but the Colonel wasn't scared. Looking at his watch, he said, "We're already four seconds behind schedule. Enough of this!" He waved his sword high in the air and whacked it down, chopping the rope in two and setting the little plane free. Off it whirled, well out of reach of the snarling Bug.

"Boy, that was brave!" Katie said.

"Brave, nothing!" snapped the Colonel. "That's what this sword's for: emergencies! We can't be late, or you'll never see your flower."

"Look at that tall building!"
Katie shouted. "It reaches into the
clouds!"

"That's RAM Tower," said the
Colonel. "It's where we find the
Flower Painters and anybody else in
the computer who's got a special job
to do."

"Like you, Colonel?" Katie
asked.

"No, you silly!" the Colonel said. "I live in ROM. I'm here all the time. Those folks in RAM
Tower come and go each time your father turns on the computer."

Katie leaned over the side of the airplane. "Where are we going to land?" she asked.

"No time for that now," said the Colonel. "I'll land later and meet you on the ground. It's up to
you to get the Flower Painters. Here, put this on!" He threw her a canvas sack full of buttons and
straps. It was a parachute!

Dizzy and afraid, Katie put on the parachute and a crash helmet she found under her seat. She
climbed up on the side of the plane. "I'm not going to be a baby," she told herself. "I'm not!"

The plane dived toward RAM Tower, and the Colonel hollered, "JUMP!!" Katie leaped from the plane, counted to five, and pulled the red cord on the parachute. It ballooned open above her and slowed her fall. "BULLS-EYE!" she cried, as she landed right in front of the Flower Painters' door.

Katie ripped off the parachute and pounded on the door: "BAMM! BAMM!" The door flew open, and the Flower Painters looked out. "Come, quick!" Katie cried. "We need a flower, and the Colonel's waiting. We're so late because of that awful Bug! Please, hurry!"

The Flower Painters moved like whirlwinds. They grabbed buckets of gleaming paint and dashed out the door. They and Katie jumped onto a slippery brass pole and slid down it like firefighters on their way to a fire. "YIPPEE!" Katie yelled.

As soon as the Flower Painters hit the ground, they climbed into a bus and started the motor. "Hey! Wait for me!" Katie shouted. She jumped on the back and clambered onto the roof.

Just then, the Colonel ran up and made a giant leap onto the tail end of the bus. "Head to the CPU, then on to the Tube for some fireworks!" he yelled.

The bus entered a vast arena filled with cheering, chanting people. The smell of paint and burnt gunpowder was everywhere. The bus whizzed out to the center of the arena and stopped. Daylight vanished, and in the darkness Katie heard shouts of "WE WANT A FLOWER!! WE WANT A FLOWER!!"

The painters popped onto a wooden platform and climbed
up three ancient cannons pulled from some pirate's wreck.
Into the cannons they poured their glowing paint—RED,
BLUE, and GREEN. "Those are the same colors your TV
uses," the Colonel explained. "Mix 'em together and you can
make any color you choose."

"Stand back!! Stand back!!" the Flower Painters
screamed.

"BOOOM!! BAROOOM!! BOOOM!!" roared the cannons, belching colorful clouds of fire and smoke into the night-time sky. Far up above the ground, the colors joined and exploded into a beautiful flower. "It's a daffodil!" Katie cried, and she clapped her hands and jumped up and down. "HURRAY!!!" cheered the people in the stands.

"Thanks for all your help, Katie," said the Colonel. "You did a wonderful job, but now it's time to say good-bye."

"You're right," Katie said, "I gotta get home! But how?"

"Quick, climb into one of the cannons," the Colonel said. "We have to keep firing them, or the flower will disappear. We'll send you along with the paint. You'll be home in a flash!"

Katie raced over and gave the Colonel a great big hug. Then she climbed inside a cannon. "All ready!" she shouted.

"BOOM!!" roared the cannon. Katie flew into the sky.

Katie crashed into the picture screen. "OWWW!" she cried. Her nose stung and her eyes watered. "Darn screen," she said. On the screen was the flower. She looked around. The Colonel was gone! She was back home!

"That must have hurt!" said her father, leaning over her.

"It's okay," Katie said bravely. "I really helped the Colonel, didn't I, Dad?"

"You sure did," said her father. "Now you know how our computer works. Hey! How'd you get that paint all over you?"

"In the computer!" Katie said. "And I want to go back real soon!"

About the Author and Illustrator

FRED D'IGNAZIO is a freelance writer currently living in Roanoke, Virginia, with his wife, Janet, his two children, Catie and Eric, and his cat MOW-MOW. In addition to *Katie and the Computer,* Fred has written numerous other children's books about computers, including *The Star Wars Question & Answer Book About Computers,* and *Chip Mitchell: The Case of the Stolen Computer Brains.*

STAN GILLIAM is a freelance designer and illustrator currently living in Chapel Hill, North Carolina. He has a master's degree in Educational Media Design and has worked on several projects for children including interactive exhibits for the North Carolina Museum of Life and Science. He is also a painter who exhibits his work frequently, and a former college art instructor.

WHAT IS A COMPUTER?

A computer is a machine that follows a plan. The machine is the computer's *hardware*; the plan is its *software*.

Inside the *machine* are thousands of tiny wires—on flat plastic boards and on chips even smaller than your thumbnail. Through the wires flow charges of electricity. Sometimes *high*, sometimes *low*, these charges make up a special computer language of *ones* and *zeros*. Using this language, a computer can talk and listen, think and remember. It can play games and help you with your homework.

When you want a computer to do something, you figure out a *plan*—a list of orders to the computer. This list of orders is called a *program*. You write the program in a language like English. The computer translates your language to its machine language of ones and zeros. An example of a program you might write is the FLOWER program written by Katie's father to draw a picture of a flower on the picture screen.

MEET THE FLOWER BYTES

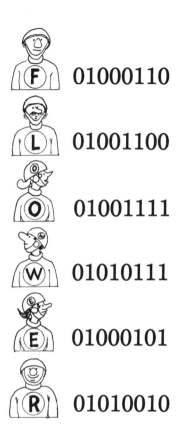

F 01000110

L 01001100

O 01001111

W 01010111

E 01000101

R 01010010

There is a Byte for every letter in the alphabet. Each Byte is made up of eight ones and zeros. To create the Bytes, the computer sends charges of electricity—a *high* charge for a *one* and a *low* charge for a *zero*.

In our story, the Colonel calls the Bytes by blowing his bugle. A "BLAATT!" from the bugle means a *one*; a "BLEEETT!" means a *zero*. Find the page in the story where the Colonel is blowing his bugle. What Byte (or *letter*) is he calling? How would he call the others?

The heart of a home computer, like the one in the story, is the *chip* — a tiny maze of microscopic wires. A real chip, like the one to the right, is only this big:

but it has enough wires to act as the computer's *brain* or its *main memory*.

The CPU, RAM, and ROM in our story are actually chips. When they are wired together, they make a home computer like the one Katie visited.

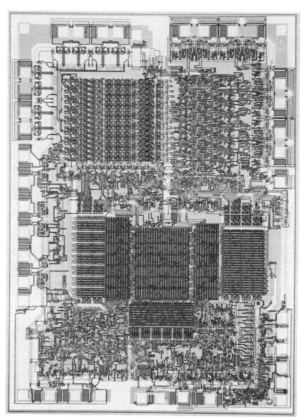

8085 CPU chip courtesy Intel Corporation

The Chip
(Hardware)

ROM
(Read Only Memory)

Home of the Control Program (The Colonel)

CPU
(Central Processing Unit)

The Computer's Brain

RAM
(Random Access Memory)

The Computer's Main Memory